HIP-HOP ARTISTS

EMINEM

RAP LEGEND

BY CARLA MOONEY

Essential Library
An Imprint of Abdo Publishing
abdobooks.com

ABDOBOOKS.COM

Published by Abdo Publishing, a division of ABDO, PO Box 398166, Minneapolis, Minnesota 55439.

Printed in the United States of America, North Mankato, Minnesota.
102021
012022

Cover Photo: Kevin Winter/ImageDirect/Getty Images Entertainment/Getty Images
Interior Photos: Denis Doyle/AP Images, 4; Paul Warner/WireImage/Getty Images, 7; Shutterstock Images, 11, 13, 39, 81; Allstar Picture Library Ltd./Alamy, 14, 31; Andrey Bayda/Shutterstock Images, 17; JJs/Alamy, 20; Fryderyk Gabowicz/picture-alliance/dpa/AP Images, 22; Carlos Osorio/AP Images, 25, 63; Bill Pugliano/Getty Images Entertainment/Getty Images, 27; Stephen Trupp/Star Max/AP Images, 34; Ron Frehm/AP Images, 42; Peter Kramer/Star Max/AP Images, 44; Suzanne Plunkett/AP Images, 47; Kevork Djansezian/AP Images, 51; AA Film Archive/Alamy, 54–55; Joe Seer/Shutterstock Images, 56; Chris Pizzello/AP Images, 58; SMA/Shannon McCollum/Wenn/Newscom, 61; Pierre Barlier/Abaca Press/Alamy, 67; Yui Mok/AP Images, 68; Lucy Nicholson/Reuters/Newscom, 70; Sonja van Kampen/Geisler-Fotopre/picture-alliance/dpa/AP Images, 74–75; Sthanlee B. Mirador/Sipa USA/AP Images, 78; Eli Wilson/Shutterstock Images, 85; Kim Kelley-Wagner/Shutterstock Images, 87; Chris Pizzello/Invision/AP Images, 88; MPIMIcelotta/MediaPunch/IPX/AP Images, 92; Amy Harris/Invision/AP Images, 94–95; Dennis Van Tine/MediaPunch/IPX/AP Images, 96

Editor: Arnold Ringstad
Series Designer: Laura Graphenteen

LIBRARY OF CONGRESS CONTROL NUMBER: 2021941057

PUBLISHER'S CATALOGING-IN-PUBLICATION DATA

Names: Mooney, Carla, author.
Title: Eminem: rap legend / by Carla Mooney
Other title: rap legend
Description: Minneapolis, Minnesota : Abdo Publishing, 2022 | Series: Hip-hop artists | Includes online resources and index.
Identifiers: ISBN 9781532196140 (lib. bdg.) | ISBN 9781098217952 (ebook)
Subjects: LCSH: Eminem (Marshall Mathers), 1972---Juvenile literature. | Rap musicians--United States--Biography--Juvenile literature. | Rap (Music)--Juvenile literature. | Lyricists--Biography--Juvenile literature.
Classification: DDC 782.421649--dc23

CONTENTS

Chapter ONE

DISCOVERY AT THE RAP OLYMPICS

In 1997, a young rapper named Eminem arrived in Los Angeles, California, for the Rap Olympics. This competition for up-and-coming MCs, or rappers, featured both team and individual competitions. One of the event's sponsors was Wendy Day, the CEO of artists advocacy group the Rap Coalition. Day had first met Eminem at a music industry event, where he had given her one of his recordings. Day later heard the young rapper perform in New York, and she loved his unique style. She had never seen anyone quite like him before. Day invited him to compete on the Rap Coalition team.

By the time he arrived at the Rap Olympics, Eminem had hit rock bottom. He was out of money, had just lost his job, and had been evicted from his home. Eminem was

Eminem's artistry at improvising lyrics and his skill in delivering them caught the attention of music industry executives.

FREESTYLE RAP

Freestyle rap, or freestyling, is a type of improvisational rap by artists or groups that is often used in competition. Freestyle generally describes rap lyrics that are created on the spot without having been written prior to a performance. Freestyle raps are often performed a cappella, without any backup. Sometimes, artists will freestyle over beatboxing or an instrumental version of a song. Freestyling in a group setting is called a cypher. To prove that lyrics are being made up on the spot, artists will often include mentions of the location or people around them when they are freestyling.

desperate to win the competition and bring home the $500 prize. His manager, Paul Rosenberg, encouraged him to do his best but told him not to worry if he did not win.

CRUSHING THE COMPETITION

In the individual competition, Eminem took the stage against other rappers. In each round, two rappers took turns freestyling lyrics to see who had the better verse, flow, and delivery. Eminem stunned the audience with his sharp, tongue-twisting, boastful rhymes. "He was unbelievable," says Rosenberg. "I was sitting in there next to this big black guy, and after the first round, he shouted, 'Just give it to the white boy, it's over. Just give it to the white boy.'"[1]

Paul Rosenberg, *right*, began working with Eminem in the late 1990s and frequently appears in skits on the rapper's albums.

In the individual finals, Eminem faced another talented freestyle MC. Although many in the audience believed Eminem should have won, he came in second place. "I went in there just [attacking] everyone, man," Eminem says about the Rap Olympics. "I had nothing to lose. I took second place and I was very unused to that. . . . And I was so mad. Steaming, dog. I had nowhere to live back home.

The winner of Rap Olympics got, like five hundred dollars. I could have used that, man. Second place got nothing."[2]

Rosenberg was more optimistic. "I knew that even though he didn't [win], it was great for us—it was exposure we could turn into something," he says.[3] Rosenberg was right. Eminem may not have won the Rap Olympics, but he did grab the attention of two employees of Interscope Records, Dean Geistlinger and Evan Bogart.

INTERSCOPE RECORDS

In 1989, film producer Ted Field and record producer Jimmy Iovine formed Interscope Records as a small, alternative label. In 1990, Warner Music Group purchased a 50 percent interest in the company to market and distribute its music. In 1992, rap label Death Row Records made a deal for Interscope to distribute Death Row's music. In 1992, Death Row Records released Dr. Dre's album *The Chronic*. In 1993, Interscope and Death Row released Snoop Dogg's debut album, *Doggystyle*. In 1996, MCA, Inc. (later known as Universal Music Group or UMG) bought Interscope Records. By 2004, Interscope had become one of UMG's biggest labels.

INTEREST FROM INTERSCOPE

After the competition, Geistlinger and Bogart approached Rosenberg and Eminem. They loved Eminem's style and performance and asked for a demo tape. Eminem gave them a copy of his latest recording, *The Slim Shady EP*. EP stands for extended play. It included seven songs, two of which were shortened radio versions of other songs on the album. The following day, Eminem freestyled on a local radio show with other rappers from the competition. Then he flew back home to Detroit, Michigan.

Meanwhile, Geistlinger and Bogart gave Eminem's tape to legendary record producer Jimmy Iovine, president of Interscope Records. After hearing the young rapper, Iovine brought the tape to Dr. Dre. Dre was a superstar rapper who had come to fame in the group N.W.A, a pioneering act in the gangsta rap genre. He was also a music producer. On hearing the tape, Dre immediately recognized Eminem's voice from the radio appearance following the Rap Olympics. Dre had been

DR. DRE

Born Andre Romelle Young, Dr. Dre got his start in music working as a DJ as a teen. He achieved his first significant success with the rap group N.W.A, which also included rappers Arabian Prince, Eazy-E, and Ice Cube. N.W.A's lyrics were harsh and depicted life on the streets. The group released its debut studio album, *Straight Outta Compton*, in 1988. Its release marked the beginning of a new genre: gangsta rap. The group's second studio album, *N—4Life*, became the first hard-core rap album to reach the top of the *Billboard* 200 sales charts. In 1991, Dre cofounded Death Row Records. In 1992, he released his first solo album, *The Chronic*, which hit the top of the charts. Dre has also been influential as a producer and record executive, helping launch the careers of many rap and hip-hop artists, including Eminem and 50 Cent.

listening, and now he heard the same voice on the demo. "I was at Jimmy's house and he played the tape for me," Dre says. "He asked me what I thought of it and I said, 'Find him. Now.' I thought the tape was incredible, know what I'm saying? In my entire career in the music industry, I've never found anything from a demo tape. Usually somebody knew somebody or someone was brought up to the studio. When I heard it, I didn't even know he was white. The content turned me on more than anything, and the way he was flipping it. Dark comedy is what I call it. It was incredible, I had to meet him right away."[4]

DR. DRE CALLS

When Paul Rosenberg broke the news to Eminem in early 1998, the rapper was shocked. "When Paul told me that Dre called, I was like, 'Get the f— out of here, man.' I thought he was lying. We had gotten jerked around by so many labels by that point," says Eminem.[5]

Meeting Dre at the Interscope offices was a dream come true for Eminem. He was awestruck by the gangsta rap legend.

"Eminem comes in in this bright yellow . . . sweatsuit, hoodie, pants, everything . . . it's bright . . . yellow, and I'm like, 'wow.'"[6]

—Dr. Dre, remembering his first impression of Eminem

Dr. Dre, *left*, and Jimmy Iovine, *right*, played key roles in discovering Eminem and bringing him to a mainstream audience.

"I'm looking at Dre like: 'Dude, I see you on TV all the time—you one of my biggest influences ever in life,'" he says.[7] Soon after his arrival, Eminem signed with Dre's Interscope subsidiary, Aftermath Entertainment.

Gangsta rap artists, such as 2Pac, were popular in the mid-1990s and influenced Eminem as he developed his rap career.

It was the beginning of a prolific partnership. On their first day together in the studio, Dre and Eminem recorded several songs in only a few hours. "We clicked," says Eminem. "First day in the studio, we knocked off three songs in six hours. He said he'd never done that but I was anxious to show him what I could do. I loved hip-hop so much, knew and appreciated the history of hip-hop, and I always wanted to have a voice in hip-hop. This is the goal I'd worked towards all my life."[8]

As Dre and Eminem worked together on an album, buzz began to build about the young white rapper. He was well on his way to becoming a star.

GANGSTA RAP

Gangsta rap is a style of hip-hop that uses its lyrics to show the violent experiences of inner-city youth. The genre evolved from hip-hop in the early 1980s and features harsh lyrics and hard-hitting beats. The content of these songs includes drive-by shootings, gang violence, substance abuse, misogyny, materialism, and more. Some people have criticized the genre for its violent themes. However, the artists have defended their lyrics as simply a window into the real hardships they faced growing up. Notable gangsta rap artists include N.W.A, Ice-T, Snoop Dogg, 50 Cent, Ice Cube, and 2Pac.

2PAC
2pac
GREATEST HITS
still down?
[remember me
7243 8 45374 2 5
(7243 8 45375 2 4)
LC 3098
Bel/Biem/SIAE
MADE IN ITALY
ALL RIGHTS OF THE PRODUCER AND OF THE

8 MILE
MOBILE

Chapter TWO

THE EARLY YEARS

On October 17, 1972, Marshall Mathers III entered the world. His parents, Debbie Mathers-Briggs and Marshall Mathers Jr., shared an interest in music. They performed together in a band called Daddy Warbucks, which played at motels near the border between the Dakotas and Montana. The couple married in 1970, when Debbie was only 15 years old and Mathers Jr. was 22. Their only son, Marshall Mathers III, was born two years later in Saint Joseph, Missouri.

The relationship between Debbie and Mathers Jr. did not last long, and the couple broke up when Marshall was still a baby. Mathers Jr. moved to California and had little to do with his son. As a teen, Marshall reached out to his father in several letters but received no response. Debbie was left to raise Marshall alone.

Later in his career, Eminem would fictionalize his time growing up in Detroit in his film *8 Mile*.

EMINEM'S FATHER REACHES OUT

As Eminem became a worldwide celebrity in 2001, his father attempted to reach out to him. Mathers had been working construction in California and had become the father of two more children. One of them told Mathers that there was a new rising rapper with the same name. When Mathers saw the picture of Debbie with Eminem as a child in *Rolling Stone*, he knew that the famous rapper Eminem was his son. Mathers published an open letter to his son in an issue of the *Mirror* in which he apologized for abandoning his child and asked Eminem to contact him. Eminem ignored the request. In a 2010 interview, Eminem said that he had no desire ever to meet his father. Mathers died in 2019 without reuniting with his son.

MOVES AND UPHEAVAL

Debbie struggled to hold down a job for more than a few months. She and Marshall moved frequently between Missouri and Michigan. When the money ran out, they lived with family and friends. The constant upheaval was hard on young Marshall. "I would change schools two, three times a year," he says. "That was probably the roughest part about it all."[1] The constant moving made it difficult for Marshall to make friends. At each new school, he generally kept to himself and was treated as an outsider. He was also often the target of bullies. "Beat up in [the] bathroom, beat up in the hallways, shoved

Marshall spent much of his childhood in and around Detroit, Michigan.

into lockers. You know, just for, you know, for the most part . . . just bein' the new kid," he says.[2]

One time, a school bully beat ten-year-old Marshall so badly on the playground he suffered a cerebral hemorrhage and slipped into a coma. For the next five days, Marshall drifted in and out of the coma. When he finally came to, doctors told his mother that the boy might not survive. Despite the doctors' grim prediction, Marshall pulled through. He would later describe the trauma in the song "Brain Damage" on his breakthrough 1999 album, *The Slim Shady LP*. LP stands for long play.

SETTLING IN DETROIT

In 1986, Marshall's mother gave birth to his half brother, Nathan. Around the same time, the family settled in East Detroit, Michigan. In East Detroit, Eight Mile Road formed a geographic and demographic barrier between upper- and middle-class neighborhoods on one side and working-class neighborhoods on the other. Marshall's family lived on the rough side of Eight Mile in a mostly Black neighborhood.

Sometimes Marshall experienced problems being one of the few white people living in his neighborhood. "Most of the time it was relatively cool, but I would get beat up sometimes when I'd walk around the neighborhood and kids didn't know me. One day I got jumped by, like, six dudes for no reason. I also got shot at, and ended

EIGHT MILE ROAD

For decades, Eight Mile Road in Detroit has been a main road for commuters and area residents. More than 1,500 businesses are located along Eight Mile Road. However, along its poorer sections, Eight Mile Road is an impoverished and dangerous area. Struggling businesses and broken windows litter the road. It is also common to find prostitutes, drug addicts, seedy bars, and strip clubs in these areas. Since 1993, the Eight Mile Boulevard Association, a nonprofit organization, has worked to improve and promote Eight Mile Road for transportation, businesses, and residents.

up running out of my shoes, crying. I was 15 years old and I didn't know how to handle that [stuff]," he says.[3]

"It was the energy—you could just say what you wanna say. You could talk about your life and talk about [stuff] that bothers you. I just gravitated toward it and never strayed from the first day I heard a rap song."[4]

—Eminem, talking about his interest in rap music

DISCOVERING RAP MUSIC

As a child, Marshall was drawn to storytelling. He dreamed of becoming a comic book artist one day. When he was about nine years old, his uncle Ronnie gave him the soundtrack from the 1984 movie *Breakin'*, a break dancing–themed musical film. On the soundtrack, Marshall listened to his first rap song, "Reckless," which featured rapper Ice-T. Ronnie introduced him to more of the most popular rap songs. Marshall was drawn to the hip-hop style and soon began listening to all the hip-hop

UNCLE RONNIE'S DEATH

In 1991, Marshall was devastated when he learned that his uncle Ronnie had died by suicide. For days, Marshall didn't talk. He could not bring himself to attend the funeral. He admits that he still doesn't understand why Ronnie decided to take his own life. To remember his uncle, Marshall has his name, Ronnie, tattooed on his arm.

FOR THE BREAK OF YOUR LIFE!
Breakin'
Push it to pop it!
Rock it to lock it!
Break it to make it!
Featuring the hottest break dancers in Americ
Shabba-doo,
Boogaloo Shrimp,
and the amazing 9-year-old sensation Coco!
THE CANNON GROUP, INC. Presents A GOLAN-GLOBUS Production "BREAKIN'" Starring LUCINDA DICKEY "SHABBA-D
"BOOGALOO SHRIMP" BEN LOKEY PHINEAS NEWBORN III and CHRISTOPHER McDONALD Director of Photography HANANIA
Musical Numbers Staged and Choreographed by JAIME ROGERS Executive Producers MENAHEM GOLAN and YORAM GLOBUS
Story by CHARLES PARKER & ALLEN DeBEVOISE Screenplay by CHARLES PARKER & ALLEN DeBEVOISE and GERALD

The soundtrack to the 1984 film *Breakin'* introduced Marshall to rap, changing the direction of his life.

and rap he could find, especially music by groups such as the Beastie Boys and N.W.A.

Marshall quickly became absorbed with rap music's energy and excitement. He had found an interest that helped him get through the struggle and loneliness of his childhood years. The songs' tough-talking lyrics and street-smart sound gave Marshall a voice. "What got me through this phase of my life was rapping. I found something," he says.[5]

THE BEASTIE BOYS

One of Eminem's early rap influences was the American hip-hop group the Beastie Boys. Their 1986 debut album, *Licensed to Ill*, reached the top of the *Billboard* charts. It became the first rap album to reach Number 1 in the United States and would spend 73 weeks on the *Billboard* 200. *Licensed to Ill* was one of the first hip-hop albums with mainstream appeal. It introduced white kids in the suburbs to hip-hop music and showed the industry that rap music could be commercially successful.

Miller

Chapter THREE

RAP BATTLES AND PERSONAL TROUBLES

As a teen, Marshall's interest in rap intensified. He spent hours studying the styles of different rappers. "I'd go to friends' houses and rap, or I'd stay in my room all day, standing by the mirror and lip-syncing songs, trying on different clothes, trying to look cool. I knew every song by LL [Cool J] and Run-DMC and the Beastie Boys," he says.[1]

SCHOOL DAYS

While Marshall spent hours studying rap, he did not have nearly the same interest in school. He attended Lincoln High School in Warren, Michigan, where he struggled in most of his classes. English, however, was one of his better subjects. He read the dictionary so he could learn more words and make better rhymes in his raps. "I found that no

The New York rap group the Beastie Boys was a major inspiration to Marshall as he was getting into rap.

matter how bad I was at school, like and no matter how low my grades might have been at some times, I always was good at English. . . . I just felt like I wanna be able to have all of these words at my disposal, in my vocabulary at all times whenever I need to pull 'em out," he says.[2]

As a young teen, Marshall met someone who would become one of his best friends, DeShaun "Proof" Holton. The two teens shared a love of rap and hip-hop music. They traded rhymes and listened to the latest music and rappers together.

Proof went to nearby Osborn High School, where most of the students were Black. At lunchtime, Proof would sneak Marshall into the Osborn High cafeteria. There, Marshall tested his rap skills in lunchtime rap battles. The battles pitted two rappers against each other in a head-to-head contest of words. To be successful, a rapper needed to be quick and skilled with words and rhymes. At first, the Osborn students thought the young white rapper would be easy to beat. But all of Marshall's hours of practice and study were starting to pay off. "Then Em would come out and kill the whole lunchroom," says Proof.[3]

Meanwhile, Marshall's schoolwork continued to slide. He started skipping school and failing his classes.

He ended up failing ninth grade and repeated his freshman year. Eventually, Marshall flunked ninth grade three times before dropping out of school entirely in 1989.

Proof and Marshall would remain friends and collaborators for several years after meeting in high school.

MARSHALL AND KIM

When he was about 15 years old, Marshall met a freshman named Kimberly Scott at a house party. Kim had left home with her sister to escape an alcoholic stepfather and was living in a youth shelter outside of Detroit. The two teens shared similar troubles, and they hit it off right away. Before long, Marshall brought Kim home to live with him and his mother.

Eventually, Marshall and Kim began dating and spending most of their time together. Over the years, their relationship was often chaotic. According to Marshall's mother, Debbie, his relationship with Kim was consuming and exhausting. "She wound him up, and they had the most terrible rows. I had to break up the cursing between them. The girl

RAP BATTLES

In a rap battle, two rappers get on the stage and take turns rapping in a war of words. As the crowd listens, the rappers trade rhymes and insults. Each one tries to come up with the smartest rhymes and best insults. Often, the rap war of words becomes personal and vulgar. Sometimes, the rappers perform with a beat. Other times, they perform without one. By the end, the audience crowns a winner with their cheers or boos.

thrives on confrontation. But Marshall was never violent towards her," she says.[4]

When Marshall dropped out of school at age 17, Debbie kicked him and Kim out of her house. To support himself and Kim, Marshall took on various jobs to

Marshall and Kim broke up and got back together multiple times over the years.

earn money. They moved around a lot, often living in seedy neighborhoods full of crime and drugs. Thieves regularly broke into their place and stole televisions, clothing, and whatever else they could take.

In 1995, Kim unexpectedly became pregnant. Kim and Marshall's daughter, Hailie Jade Mathers, was born on December 25, 1995. With the newborn, the couple moved back in with Marshall's mother. Yet peace was elusive, and the couple clashed with Debbie repeatedly. To support Kim and the baby, Marshall took a job working as a dishwasher and short-order cook at a restaurant called Gilbert's Lodge. His boss, Pete Karagiaouris, remembers that Marshall was a good worker most of the time. In the kitchen, he would often rap all the orders. Sometimes the manager had to tell Marshall to quiet down.

Marshall didn't want Hailie to grow up as he had, constantly moving from place to place and worrying about whether the family had enough money. However, the pressures of supporting his family and his struggles to build a career caused problems in his relationship with Kim. Over and over, the explosive couple fought, broke up, and reconciled. They would get married in June 1999, only to divorce in 2001.

RAPPING ONSTAGE

Throughout the upheaval in his personal life, Marshall continued to pursue his dream of becoming a rapper. He got together with other rap friends and recorded tracks in one friend's basement. While working with other rappers on their music, Marshall started showing them what he called the inside rhyme. At the time, most rappers put together two lines that rhymed and left it at that. Marshall took it up a notch and tried to put as many words that rhymed as he could into a single line.

VANILLA ICE

When Marshall was a teen, a white rapper named Vanilla Ice rose to fame. Born Robert Van Winkle, Vanilla Ice released his first album in 1989 and shot to fame with the single "Ice Ice Baby." The catchy tune caught on with audiences and radio stations. Soon, Vanilla Ice became a pop idol, promoting products and touring with rapper MC Hammer. In interviews, Vanilla Ice talked about his difficult childhood and growing up on the streets. However, when journalists investigated his claims, they discovered he had exaggerated or made up many facts. The controversy damaged Vanilla Ice's credibility and career. Additionally, critics said that his lyrics had little creativity or originality. Marshall believed that Vanilla Ice made it more difficult for future white rappers like himself to get respect in the industry.

When Marshall was ready to take his rhymes out of the basement, he found few audiences willing to listen to a skinny white guy. So he decided to enter rap battles at local clubs. The battles would give him the opportunity to sharpen his skills and challenge other rappers on the open stage.

In Detroit, Marshall and Proof frequented open-mic contests at the Hip Hop Shop. When he rapped, Marshall first adopted the name M&M from his initials. Eventually, M&M morphed into Eminem. When Eminem took the stage, the mostly Black audience usually booed him. Once they heard him rhyme, the boos quickly stopped. "I had to work up to a certain level before people would even look past my color. . . . But as time went on, I started to get respect," he says.[5] Slowly, the Detroit locals began to recognize that the young white rapper had talent.

As Eminem gained respect in the Detroit rap scene, he received offers to join several rap groups. He rapped with the New Jacks and Soul Intent before forming his own rap

THE HIP HOP SHOP

Located on Seven Mile Road on the west side of Detroit, the Hip Hop Shop was opened in 1993 by fashion designer Maurice Malone. The boutique became a hub for hip-hop culture in the 1990s. The Hip Hop Shop became famous for hosting rap battles every Saturday afternoon. The rap battles often featured Detroit rappers early in their careers, including Eminem, Slum Village, and others. The Hip Hop Shop closed its doors in 1997. Today, it sells merchandise through an online store.

The film *8 Mile* later depicted the kinds of rap battles in which Marshall started to show off his talent before audiences.

group, D12, with Proof and four other friends.

RECORDING IN THE STUDIO

Eminem's first break occurred when local music producer Marky Bass heard him freestyling. Bass invited

> "I finally found something that yeah, this kid over here, you know, he may have more chicks, and he may, you know, have better clothes, or whatever, but he can't do this like me. . . . He can't write what I'm writing right now. And it started to feel like, you know, maybe Marshall's gettin' a little respect."[6]
>
> *–Eminem*

Eminem into the studio to rhyme and record. "He was phenomenal," Bass says. "I dropped everything I was doing and I put everything I had into this kid."[7]

Bass helped Eminem record his first album, *Infinite.* Eminem recorded the album's tracks right before his daughter was born. On them, he rapped about love, unity, and overcoming hard times. He modeled his rhyming and style after other popular hip-hop artists at the time, such as Nas and AZ.

D12

The Dirty Dozen, also known as D12, is an American hip-hop group from Detroit, Michigan. Formed in 1996, the group included six of Detroit's best underground rappers: Proof, Bizarre, Eminem, Kon Artis, Bugz, and Kuniva. The name Dirty Dozen represents the six members plus their six alter egos. D12 released its debut album, *Devil's Night*, in 2001. The group followed up with the release of *D12 World* in 2004. In 2005, D12 joined the Anger Management Tour with Eminem, 50 Cent, G-Unit, and Lil Jon.

Bass's Web Entertainment released *Infinite* in 1996. In trying to model himself after other artists, Eminem had lost the sharp wit and pent-up rage that made his music and lyrics stand out. "I've always been a [smart aleck] comedian, and that's why it wasn't a good album," Eminem admits.[8] Radio stations and DJs largely ignored *Infinite* and didn't play it. Nothing stood out on the album. The album failed to make a profit and sold fewer than 1,000 copies.[9] "That first album was very different from what he's doing now," said Rosenberg in 2000. "He was just starting out and he was trying to get airplay, so he made a record that he thought would fit in with what was happening at the time in rap. The songs were a little more upbeat."[10]

The disappointing reaction to *Infinite* was only one in a series of setbacks for Eminem. Right before his daughter's first birthday, he lost his cooking job at Gilbert's Lodge. In 1997, he and Kim had another bad breakup. He moved back in with his mother and began using drugs and alcohol more frequently. At one point, he tried to take his own life with an overdose of Tylenol. Eventually, Eminem would turn all of his pain, anger, and disappointment into material for his music.

Chapter FOUR

"I'M SLIM SHADY"

After the failure of *Infinite*, Eminem decided to stop trying to fit in as a rapper. Instead, he would make the kind of music he wanted. That's also when he started to experiment with a new character: Slim Shady.

SLIM SHADY IS BORN

In the summer of 1997, the character of Slim Shady emerged. Marshall already had an alias as a rapper, Eminem, which he used both on- and offstage. The character of Slim Shady, however, was different. He emerged at a point when everything in Eminem's life seemed to be broken, from his rocky relationship with Kim to the disappointing sales for *Infinite*. According to the rapper, Debbie's prescription drug abuse caused erratic mood swings and repeated fights at home.

Developing his Slim Shady character and joining forces with Dr. Dre helped take Eminem's career to the next level.

Eminem's friend Proof encouraged the members of D12 to create alter egos and experiment with writing lyrics as those characters. Using a character allowed the group's members to create hard-core, abrasive raps.

For Eminem, Slim Shady provided a much-needed outlet for his emotions, frustration, and rage. Once the idea of Shady came to him, Eminem created a list of words that rhymed with Shady and immediately started writing. "The more I started writing and the more I slipped into this Slim Shady character, the more it just started becoming me. My true feelings were coming out, and I just needed an outlet to dump them in. I needed some type of persona. I needed an excuse to let go of all the rage," he says.[1]

> **"Slim Shady is a name for my temper or anger. Eminem is just the rapper, Slim Shady is the attitude behind him, and Marshall Mathers is who I am at the end of the day."[2]**
>
> *—Eminem*

As Slim Shady, Eminem wrote about his troubled relationship with his mother. He described his problems with Kim. He raged about his rough upbringing and the dead-end jobs he felt trapped in. Using this new persona, Eminem created furious rhymes about destruction, drugs, rape, murder, and inner-city life. In Slim Shady's voice, the lyrics and rhymes flowed. Within weeks, Eminem had written several new songs.

In 1997, Eminem released *The Slim Shady EP*, consisting of seven songs. On this album, the rapper showed some of the characteristics for which he would become famous, including his rapid-fire, nasal delivery and his violent lyrics. In the lyrics, he also showcased his dark and snarky sense of humor.

Meanwhile, Eminem's open-mic performances in Detroit had caught the attention of Paul Rosenberg, a lawyer who loved rap music. He had signed on as Eminem's manager. When he heard the new, more hard-core music on *The Slim Shady EP*, Rosenberg was excited. He passed Eminem's demo tape to multiple record executives. Rosenberg also entered Eminem in several rap competitions. One of those competitions was the 1997 Rap Olympics in Los Angeles that got him noticed by Interscope Records and eventually, rap legend Dr. Dre.

THE SLIM SHADY LP

Over several months, Eminem worked with Dr. Dre on his new project, *The Slim Shady LP*. Several of the songs from *The Slim Shady EP* landed on the new album. With Dre's

An expanded edition of *The Slim Shady LP* was released to celebrate the groundbreaking album's twentieth anniversary.

touch, the new album had a higher sound quality and better instrumentation than Eminem's previous recordings. Eminem also credits Dre with helping him become a better rapper. "Dre made me better," he says. "He showed me how to deliver rhymes over a beat, and he showed me that you stick with something until you have it just how you want it."[3]

"BRAIN DAMAGE" LAWSUIT

In 2001, sanitation worker DeAngelo Bailey sued Eminem for $1 million. Bailey accused the rapper of invading his privacy for writing about him in the song "Brain Damage" on *The Slim Shady LP*. The song portrays Bailey as a violent school bully. Although Bailey admitted to pushing Eminem in elementary school, he said it wasn't that bad. In 2003, a judge dismissed the lawsuit and ruled that it was clear to the public that the rapper had exaggerated his lyrics.

Dre's experience as a successful rapper and producer gave Eminem's new album instant credibility within the music industry. With Dre's backing, Eminem began to generate more buzz in the rap scene. When *The Slim Shady LP* was released in February 1999, it entered the pop music charts at Number 2. Within two weeks, the album sold 480,000 copies.[4]

EMINEM
THE
Slim Shady
LP
DISC 1
(THE ALBUM)
AFTERMATH
INTERSCOPE
UMe
WEB
00602577637445 CD01
All Rights Reserved. Unauthorized copying

The breakout album set the tone for Eminem's career. Critics praised Eminem for his sharp lyrics, dark humor, and unique style. Stephen Thomas Erlewine, a critic with AllMusic, wrote, "Eminem's supreme gifts are an expansive vocabulary and vivid imagination, which he unleashes with wicked humor and unsparing anger in equal measure."[5] Most of the album's songs centered on topics many teens could relate to, such as being broke or getting beaten up. In Slim Shady's world, every person who wronged him was on the receiving end of violent revenge. Through it all, Eminem added a layer of humor in his songs' violence and anger.

The album also invited controversy. Critics expressed outrage over the disturbingly violent imagery found in many songs. They called Eminem a homophobe, a misogynist, and an advocate of domestic violence. Eminem offered

DEBBIE FILES A LAWSUIT

Eminem's mother, Debbie Mathers-Briggs, was upset by *The Slim Shady LP* and the rapper's claims in the album's songs that she used drugs. She filed a $10 million slander lawsuit against her son. Debbie vehemently denied that she used drugs when Eminem was growing up. Eventually, the lawsuit was settled in 2001 for $25,000. After paying her lawyers, Debbie was left with a little more than $1,600.[6]

no apologies for his music or lyrics. He pointed out that the album wasn't meant for younger kids and that it came with a parental advisory sticker. He explained that he was not, and never intended to be, a role model for kids.

To promote the album, Eminem did more than 100 interviews with various media outlets. He toured constantly and performed his new material. Audiences instantly connected with the music, and less than two months after the album's release, *Rolling Stone* featured Eminem on its cover. "I can't say I thought the album would do as well as it did, but I could see the response as soon as Eminem started doing shows," says Rosenberg. "He connects with his audience. They identify with the rebellion. No matter what

"It was groundbreaking. It was life changing. It switched gears for hip hop forever."[7]

—Denaun Porter, member of D12, talking about The Slim Shady LP

VIDEO PREMIERE

In January 1999, the music video for "My Name Is," the lead single on *The Slim Shady LP*, premiered on MTV. The video begins with a family watching television when a show starring "Marshall Mathers" comes on. In the video, Eminem playfully impersonates several sitcom actors and celebrities. Dr. Dre appears in a short cameo as a doctor in the video. At the 1999 MTV Video Music Awards, Eminem won the award for Best New Artist in a Video for "My Name Is."

part of the country or on what side of the tracks a kid grows up, he's got something he's upset about—whether it's a rich kid whose parent won't let him go out on the weekend, or a poor kid not having what the rich kid has."[8]

The Slim Shady LP was both a commercial and critical success. After debuting at Number 2 on the *Billboard* 200 music chart, it stayed on the chart for 105 weeks.[9]

Eminem took home the award for Best New Artist in a Video at the 1999 MTV Video Music Awards, winning for "My Name Is" from *The Slim Shady LP*.

By April 1999, *The Slim Shady LP* had sold over one million copies and was certified platinum. The first single on the album, "My Name Is," reached Number 36 on the *Billboard* Hot 100 chart.[10]

After the album's successful release, Eminem and his manager, Paul Rosenberg, founded Shady Records. The new record label would specialize in hip-hop music.

At the 42nd Grammy Awards in 2000, Eminem brought home two awards: one for the Best Rap Solo Performance for "My Name Is" and another for Best Rap Album for *The Slim Shady LP*. By November 2000, the album was certified quadruple platinum. It helped to lift Eminem from an underground rapper to a well-known celebrity.

TROUBLE WITH THE LAW

In June 2000, Eminem allegedly saw his wife, Kim Scott, outside of a Michigan nightclub kissing another man. The man was an acquaintance of the couple, rapper John Guerra. Eminem allegedly hit Guerra with an unloaded pistol and threatened to kill him. Police arrested Eminem and soon after Guerra filed a lawsuit against the rapper. Eminem gave his side of the story in the track "The Kiss (Skit)" on 2002's *The Eminem Show*. He later settled the lawsuit with Guerra for $100,000. Under the settlement agreement, neither man admitted liability or wrongdoing. In the legal system, Eminem entered a plea bargain agreement in which he pleaded guilty to carrying a concealed weapon, but the assault charge was dropped. Eminem received two years' probation.

Chapter FIVE

WORLDWIDE SUCCESS AND BACKLASH

Within a year, Eminem had gone from being a Detroit nobody to being a world-famous hip-hop star. His sharp and funny rhymes and outrageous humor had won over record executives and rap listeners alike, making him one of the most talked-about rappers in the United States. While *The Slim Shady LP* launched Eminem's success in the music industry, his next album proved that he had staying power, establishing him as one of rap's great artists.

BACK TO THE STUDIO

Working with Dr. Dre again, Eminem wrote and recorded *The Marshall Mathers LP* in two months of intense and

The year 2000 brought new industry recognition, new releases, and new controversies, pushing Eminem's career to new heights.

sometimes drug-fueled creative work. Describing his work process, he later said:

> *I'm focused when I'm recording. When I record I slip into the zone. I don't like to talk a lot. I like to stick to myself and get my thoughts together, think how I'm gonna map out each song. Each song is fairly easy to write. I record vocals on one day and take the tape home to listen to them overnight. Then I do more vocals the next day. I always do my vocals twice. I might have the skeleton down, the vocals and the beat, for two months before I think of the finishing touches to put on it, like sound effects, or if I want the beat to drop out right here.*[1]

The Marshall Mathers LP showed off Eminem's writing skills and emotional range. It was darker and more personal than his previous album. He was now less of a youthful joker and more of a disgruntled grown-up. In his songs, Eminem expressed his reaction to becoming an overnight celebrity. He lashed out at the media and his loss of privacy. He flung rhymes and insults in many directions. He spouted hateful and disturbing fantasies in which he committed murders. And he delivered all of it with his trademark singsong rap. "I am always shocked by the stuff that comes out of his mouth," says Dr. Dre about Eminem. "I can't censor or stop him from saying anything. In fact, I encourage him. Together we do stuff that nobody else can even think of doing, that nobody else has the guts to do or say."[2] Rather than backing away from controversy, Eminem embraced it. By pushing boundaries in his music, he became a bigger villain and also a bigger star.

The Marshall Mathers LP **cemented Eminem's reputation for dark themes, complex wordplay, and a twisted sense of humor.**

Released in May 2000, *The Marshall Mathers LP* sold nearly two million copies in its first week, making it the fastest-selling rap album to date. The album debuted at Number 1 on the *Billboard* Top 200 chart. At the same time, *The Slim Shady LP* was still going strong at Number 28 in its sixty-fourth week on the chart.[3] Over the next two months, *The Marshall Mathers LP* sold more than 1.75 million copies.[4]

The album's first single, "The Real Slim Shady," soared up the charts. It peaked at Number 4 on the *Billboard* Hot 100 in the United States, making it Eminem's first single to break into the top ten.[5] In the song, Eminem took aim at several pop music celebrities, including Will Smith, Britney Spears, and Christina Aguilera. Other songs on the album used offensive terms for gay people, while one song, "Kim," graphically described the rapper killing his wife.

"It sounded like something Stephen King would write. It sounded like a horror movie."[6]

—Interscope Records founder Jimmy Iovine about Eminem's **The Marshall Mathers LP**

Music journalist Touré wrote a review of the album in *Rolling Stone* and praised the rapper's impressive skills. "He has a macabre imagination to rival Satan's and an incredible ability to create new rhyme-patterns.

He has a frightening proclivity to spit venom one moment and humor the next, and a never-ending slew of jaw-dropping punch lines. He is, simply, better than any other MC in hip-hop except for Jay-Z," Touré wrote. "*The Marshall Mathers LP* is a car-crash record: loud, wild, dangerous, out of control, grotesque, unsettling. It's also impossible to pull your ears away from."[7]

CROSSING THE BORDER

In October 2000, Eminem was scheduled to perform in Toronto, Canada, as part of the Anger Management tour. Ontario attorney general Jim Flaherty asked Canadian immigration officials to ban the American rapper from entering the country because of his violent lyrics. He argued that Eminem was likely going to perform songs that encouraged violence against women. Other critics suggested the rapper should be charged with hate crimes in Canada for encouraging violence against women in his music. Border officials did not respond, and Eminem's Toronto concert went on as planned.

OUTRAGE AND PROTESTS

Not everyone was a fan of Eminem's music. In September 2000, Lynne Cheney, the former chairwoman of the National Endowment for the Humanities, testified at a Senate hearing on how the entertainment industry was promoting violent imagery to young people. In her testimony, Cheney called out Eminem for promoting violence. "He talks about murdering and raping his mother. He talks about choking women slowly so he can hear their screams for a long time. He talks about using O.J.'s machete on women, and this is a man who is honored by the recording industry," she said.[8]

Gay rights and women's groups were also outraged by the album. When it was nominated for several Grammy awards, including Album of the Year, activists from these groups protested. They argued that the rapper's lyrics promoted violence and that his award nominations sent the wrong message to other artists and the entertainment industry. "[Eminem's] lyrics are the most homophobic and hateful that GLAAD has ever seen in the past 15 years," said Scott Seomin, entertainment media director for the Gay and Lesbian Alliance Against Defamation (GLAAD). "It's a dangerous message to record labels and other artists—you can not only get away with any type of lyrical content, you can be rewarded for it."[9]

At the Grammy Awards in February 2001, activists gathered to protest Eminem's nominations and his performance at the awards show. They marched outside the awards ceremony and carried banners and posters with messages such as "Don't Award Hate." On the

Grammy stage, Eminem surprised the audience when he performed his song "Stan" as a duet with superstar musician Elton John, who is gay. At the end of the performance, the two musicians embraced. Years later, Elton John would describe his duet with Eminem at the Grammys saying, "I was just mesmerized by you and your performance. . . . It was like seeing Mick Jagger for the first time. I hadn't really been exposed to that kind of rap

Eminem's 2001 duet with Elton John became an iconic moment in the rapper's career.

in live performance before, and it was electrifying. And when that [stuff] was thrown at you—about you being homophobic—I just thought, 'I'm not standing for this. It's nonsense.' I had to stand up and defend you. That Grammy performance was the start of a lovely friendship and I'm grateful for that."[10]

Despite the controversy, Eminem won two Grammy Awards, Best Rap Solo Performance for "The Real Slim Shady" and Best Rap Album for *The Marshall Mathers LP*. The album was also nominated for the Album of the Year award but lost to Steely Dan's *Two against Nature*. Loved or hated, Eminem had become a superstar.

"STAN"

Often regarded as one of Eminem's greatest hits, the song "Stan" tells the story of an obsessed fan. In the verses, Eminem narrates from the point of view of Stan, who claims to be Slim Shady's biggest fan. Stan idolizes Shady and becomes increasingly obsessed. In between the verses, Eminem uses Dido's vocals from "Thank You" and a new background track as the chorus. Critics were impressed by Eminem's timing and emotional delivery, as well as the rhythm of his lyrics. The award-winning music video for "Stan" solidified the song as a worldwide hit.

THE EMINEM SHOW

In 2002, Eminem released a new album, *The Eminem Show*. On the album, Eminem took a step away from his Slim Shady character, making it one of his most personal efforts to date. Highly anticipated, *The Eminem Show* debuted at Number 1 on the *Billboard* 200 chart. Hit singles included "Without Me," "Cleanin' Out My Closet," "Superman," and "Sing for the Moment."

The album was another commercial and critical success. It became the best-selling album of 2002 in the United States and worldwide. Worldwide sales of more than 27 million copies made it one of the best-selling albums of all time.[11] At the 2003 Grammy Awards, Eminem took home awards for Best Rap Album and Best Music Video for "Without Me."

PROBATION AGAIN

On June 28, 2001, a judge sentenced Eminem to one year's probation and community service and a fine of about $2,000 on weapon charges. The previous year, the rapper had gotten into an argument with a member of the hip-hop duo Insane Clown Posse outside a Michigan car stereo shop and pulled out a gun. When police arrived, the rapper was arrested and charged with carrying a concealed weapon and brandishing a firearm in public. He pleaded no contest to both charges.

BIG SCREEN DEBUT

In 2002, Eminem tackled a new challenge, starring in the movie *8 Mile*. In the semi-autobiographical film, Eminem plays the role of aspiring rapper Jimmy "B-Rabbit"

Director Curtis Hanson worked closely with Eminem on the set of *8 Mile*.

Smith Jr. The film follows Smith's struggles as he tries to pursue his dream of rapping while also dealing with racial stereotypes, trouble at home, and relationship problems. While the film is not a biography of Eminem's life, it is based on some of his experiences as an emerging rapper in Detroit. "I wanted to make a movie that concentrated on the struggle, not just of me being a white rapper," says Eminem. "But the struggle that rappers go through—period. I kinda felt like I don't want to be Elvis; I don't want to be like, 'Oh, my life, woe is me.' So we made a movie that took bits and pieces of my life, but it could be anybody, and anybody can relate to it."[12]

Curtis Hanson, the film's director, said he took a leap of faith when casting Eminem in the lead role. "He's in every scene," Hanson says. "One cannot hold the screen for a long period of time without conveying some kind of inner truth. I knew going into it that he had experience performing and also

Eminem attended the November 2002 premiere of *8 Mile* in Los Angeles.

adopting a character, Slim Shady. What I was looking for was actually the opposite of that. . . . What I needed in this story was the appearance of a complete lack of artifice.

I needed the appearance of one more or less exposing himself emotionally."[13]

Hanson's faith in Eminem paid off. The movie opened at Number 1 in the United States, earning more than $51 million in its opening weekend. It was the second-highest opening weekend ever for an R-rated movie.[14] The movie would go on to earn more than $242 million worldwide.[15]

Eminem received positive reviews for his first acting role. The film's soundtrack also received rave reviews. The movie's signature song, "Lose Yourself," became Eminem's first Number 1 hit. Beginning in November 2002, it topped the *Billboard* Hot 100 chart for 12 weeks. It also became the first rap song to win an Oscar for Best Original Song, taking home the prize at the 75th Academy Awards.

WHERE'S EMINEM?

When "Lose Yourself" won an Oscar in 2003 at the 75th Academy Awards, Eminem was nowhere to be found. In fact, the rapper had stayed home because he thought there was no way a rap song could win an Oscar. Instead, Eminem's collaborator on the song, Luis Resto, accepted the award in his place. Seventeen years later, Eminem made a surprise appearance at the Academy Awards in 2020 and performed his award-winning song to a thrilled audience.

Chapter SIX

RELAPSE AND RECOVERY

In 2004, Eminem released a new album, *Encore*. The album reunited him with several friends from D12. It sold 710,000 copies in its first three days and 1.5 million in its first week. Nine months later, *Encore* reached 11 million copies sold worldwide.[1] Although *Encore* was nominated for three Grammy awards, it did not reach the level of success that Eminem's previous albums had achieved. Reviewers commented that the album was uneven and less focused than his previous work. To some people, Eminem appeared weary. He began to hint that the *Encore* album might be his last. Behind the scenes, the rapper was struggling with addiction.

A PROBLEM WITH DRUGS

At many points in his life, Eminem used drugs and alcohol recreationally. He admits that he was often high when

Eminem made an appearance at the 2004 MTV Movie Awards ahead of the release of *Encore*.

he wrote lyrics and recorded songs. In the studio, he often took drugs before extended recording sessions. He wrote a good portion of *The Marshall Mathers LP* in Amsterdam, where drugs like marijuana and ecstasy were easy to find. Over the years, drugs and alcohol had filled an emptiness in his life, and he had also used them to deal with insomnia. Most of the time, he managed to find a balance.

Eminem's newfound fame and money did little to help his problem with drugs. "Temptation is a very difficult thing once you become famous because everything is available to you. You have access to everything you want," says Dr. Donna Rockwell, a clinical psychologist.[2] By 2002, Eminem had moved on to using a dangerous mix of prescription medications such as Valium, Ambien, and Vicodin.

In 2005, Eminem performed in concerts across the United States with other hip-hop acts, including 50 Cent and D12, in the Anger Management 3 tour. Rumors circulated that the rapper was thinking about retiring from performing. At one point, Eminem addressed the rumors and made a statement to MTV News that he was not retiring.

A BRIEF REHAB

That fall, Eminem pulled out of the tour due to exhaustion and canceled 13 dates across the United Kingdom and Europe. A few days later, he was hospitalized. There, doctors treated him for a dependency on sleep medication, along with addiction to painkillers and alcohol.

After a two-week stint in rehab, Eminem stayed close to home in Detroit. He worked in the studio on production

Eminem toured with close friend 50 Cent during the Anger Management 3 tour in 2005.

with D12 and other artists for the rest of the year. Within a week of being home, he started using prescription medications and painkillers again. At first, Eminem thought he could handle it. "When I went to rehab, I wasn't ready to go, so when I came out, I relapsed pretty much right away, within a week," he says.[3]

Although he didn't admit it at the time, the drugs also affected his creativity. "The pills I was taking, they had my mood really [messed] up," he says. "It was making me depressed, and you know, it just became a vicious cycle of depression."[4] He suffered from writer's block and started having trouble writing rhymes. "Whenever I tried to write anything down, literally I just couldn't write," he says. "I couldn't write a rhyme to save my life. I mean I could write them, they just weren't any good. Nothing was up to my standards. I was trying, but I couldn't think, I couldn't get them out."[5]

MARRIAGE AND DIVORCE

In January 2006, Eminem remarried Kim. It wasn't a surprise to those who knew the couple. They had a long history of getting together and breaking up. This time would be no different. Eighty-two days later, Eminem filed for divorce. By the end of 2006, the two reached a settlement to share custody of their daughter.

DEVASTATING NEWS

Then, on April 11, 2006, Eminem received devastating news. His best friend, DeShaun "Proof" Holton, had been shot and killed at a club. Since they first met as teens, Proof had been like a brother to Eminem. He had been there for Eminem both personally and professionally. At Proof's memorial, Eminem gave a tribute to his friend. "Without Proof, there would be a Marshall Mathers, but there would be no Eminem, there would not be a D12, and there would not be a Slim Shady," he said.[6]

Fans created a memorial outside the nightclub where Proof had been killed.

Proof's death sent Eminem into a spiral. He turned to drugs to cope with the loss of his friend. Some days he would stay in bed and take pills. He isolated himself from anyone who questioned his health. Friends tried to tell him that he had a problem, but Eminem was not willing to hear them.

METHADONE

Methadone is a strong prescription painkiller. It is part of a category of drugs called opioids. When a person takes methadone, it changes the way the brain and nervous system respond to pain so they feel relief. Methadone acts more slowly than other strong painkillers, such as morphine. A doctor may prescribe methadone for a person recovering from an injury or surgery. Sometimes it is used under a doctor's supervision to treat a heroin addiction. A methadone overdose can occur when a person takes more than the recommended amount of the medication, either accidentally or on purpose.

In December 2007, Eminem overdosed on methadone and was rushed to the hospital. When he returned home, he started using drugs again. However, this time he realized that he needed help. He began to see a rehab counselor weekly. He also reached out to Elton John, who became his sponsor. As a fellow musician who was nearly 30 years sober, John was able to help guide Eminem on the path to recovery. The two checked in with each other weekly. In the years since Hailie's birth, Eminem had adopted two more children, and he would later say that his three children were his main motivation to get sober.

GETTING SOBER

Slowly, Eminem began to create a sober routine and make real changes in his life. He turned to exercise to fight insomnia without drugs. As his mind became clearer, his writer's block began to lift. Once again, he incorporated his personal struggles into his music. "I came up with the concept of *Relapse*," he says. "The word, the actual word, just hit me one day. . . . I wasn't, like, trying to write an album about all that. I'd just been through it; it was all new to me still. But the word just hit me when I was in the car, and it got the wheels turning a little bit."[7]

Eminem had never recorded completely sober. In fact, much of his best work had been recorded while he was under the influence of one drug or another. He turned to Dr. Dre for help. The pair met in Orlando and within two weeks recorded 11 songs. For nearly a year, the two artists continued working together off and on, generating enough material to fill two full-length albums. Eminem focused on the lyrics while Dre and his team of engineers and musicians worked on the beats and music.

THE WAY I AM

In October 2008, Eminem published *The Way I Am*, an autobiography. In the book, he outlines his struggle with poverty, drugs, fame, heartbreak, and depression. He includes many stories about his path to fame and also adds a narrative about the controversies he has experienced in his life. The book includes more than 200 photographs spanning the rapper's career and reproductions of original lyric sheets.

RELEASING NEW MATERIAL

In 2009, Eminem released some of his new music on *Relapse*. The album centered on horror, drug rehabilitation, and relapse. Eminem's alter ego Slim Shady returned on the record.

Highly anticipated, the album debuted at Number 1 on the *Billboard* 200 and went on to become certified double platinum. Critics had mixed reviews of the new songs and criticized Eminem's overuse of unusual accents in the material. Even so, *Relapse* won a Grammy for Best Rap Album. The single "Crack a Bottle," featuring Dr. Dre and 50 Cent, won for Best Rap Performance by a Duo or Group.

In 2010, Eminem followed up *Relapse* with *Recovery*, his seventh studio album. *Recovery* was an autobiographical attempt to deal with his addiction and his struggles to

Like much of his work, Eminem's *Relapse* was highly autobiographical.

overcome it. The resulting album was more inspirational and gentler than previous albums. *Recovery* debuted at Number 1 on the *Billboard* 200 chart, making it Eminem's sixth consecutive Number 1 debut. The album produced the smash hit singles "Not Afraid" and "Love the Way You Lie" featuring Rihanna. In 2011 Eminem won Grammy Awards for Best Rap Album and Best Rap Solo Performance.

DEBBIE'S BOOK

Eminem's mother, Debbie Mathers-Briggs, released an account of her life with Eminem in November 2008. In *My Son Marshall, My Son Eminem*, Debbie describes her childhood, meeting Eminem's father, and her son's rise to fame from her perspective.

Chapter SEVEN

NEW MUSIC

By 2013, Eminem fans were becoming restless for new music from the rapper. Eminem did not disappoint. In a commercial that aired during the 2013 MTV Video Music Awards, he announced that his eighth studio album, *The Marshall Mathers LP 2*, would arrive on November 5, 2013. A preview of a new track from the album, "Berzerk," featured Eminem rhyming, "Let's take it back to straight hip-hop and start it from scratch. I'm about to bloody this track up, everybody get back."[1] Shady had returned.

THE MARSHALL MATHERS LP 2

By naming his new album after one of his most iconic works, Eminem set expectations high. For the most part, critics agreed that *The Marshall Mathers LP 2* met them. They praised his rapping skills and the album's production choices. Edna Gundersen reviewed the album in *USA Today*, writing that Eminem "captures the original release's wild, clever, emotional brilliance in a flurry of caustic, brazenly honest, rapid-fire rhymes and aggressive beats."[2]

Eminem's 2013 release of *The Marshall Mathers LP 2* showed that the rapper was still at the top of his game.

A GLOBAL ICON

In November 2013, Eminem received the Global Icon Award at the 2013 MTV Europe Music Awards. Given out for the first time in 2010, the award recognizes an artist's global impact on the music industry. Other recipients of the Global Icon Award have included Ozzy Osbourne, Whitney Houston, Queen, Bon Jovi, Janet Jackson, U2, and more.

Eminem had relearned how to write and record with a clear, sober mind. By this album, it seemed as if everything was finally falling into place. "Though *Relapse* and *Recovery* were chock-full of distilled, intricate rhymes, none of them was ever as swaggeringly fun as those

Eminem and Rihanna performed together at the 2014 MTV Video Music Awards.

on *TMMLP2*," wrote Eminem biographer Anthony Bozza. "Even when spewing homophobic and misogynist hate or exorcising deep-seated childhood trauma, the pure enthusiasm of his delivery on the record conveys a lust for life that had long been absent."[3]

The Marshall Mathers LP 2 debuted on the *Billboard* 200 chart at Number 1 and sold more than 792,000 copies in its first week.[4] By March 2017, the Recording Industry Association of America certified the album as quadruple platinum. The lead single, "Berzerk," was followed by two more singles, "Survival" and "Rap God." A fourth single, "The Monster," featured singer Rihanna. The duet reached Number 1 on the *Billboard* Hot 100 chart. At the 2015 Grammy Awards, Eminem won the Grammy for Best Rap Album for *The Marshall Mathers LP 2*. He won another Grammy for Best Rap/Sung Collaboration for "The Monster."

HOTSTYLZ FEUD

In 2015, rapper Raymond Jones, known as Raydio G and part of the Hotstylz rap trio, sued Eminem and Interscope Records for $8 million. He claimed that Eminem's song "Rap God" featured a 25-second sample from Hotsylz's 2007 "Lookin' Boy." Eminem disputed the accusation and insisted that he had never heard of Jones or his music. In February 2016, the two sides reached a confidential settlement agreement.

SHADY XV

In 2014, Eminem released *Shady XV*, a two-disc compilation album that included songs by various artists represented by Shady Records. The album celebrated Shady Records' fifteenth anniversary. The first disc included new songs from Shady Records artists such as D12, Slaughterhouse, Bad Meets Evil, and Yelawolf. It also included new songs from Shady Records' founder, Eminem. The second disc featured some of the label's greatest hits, including Eminem's "Lose Yourself" and 50 Cent's "In Da Club."

To promote the album, Eminem performed a nearly seven-minute freestyle rap as part of a longer freestyle video called "Cypher" that featured artists on the album. The album debuted at Number 3 on the *Billboard* chart. It received

FEUD WITH MACHINE GUN KELLY

Eminem's feud with rapper Machine Gun Kelly began back in 2012 when Kelly tweeted about Eminem's daughter Hailie. Several years later, Eminem responded on the song "Not Alike" on the album *Kamikaze*. He rapped, "I'm talkin' to you, but you already know who the f— you are, Kelly/I don't use sublims and sure as f— don't sneak-diss/But keep commenting on my daughter Hailie."[5] Kelly responded with his own diss in his song "Rap Devil." Since then, the two rappers have continued to trade insults in social media and interviews.

mixed reviews from critics. Some said that the album's new material paled in comparison to its collection of greatest hits.

REVIVAL

Eminem's ninth studio album, *Revival*, arrived on December 15, 2017, debuting at Number 1 on the *Billboard* 200 chart. It was his eighth consecutive album to top the *Billboard* chart, making Eminem the first artist to have eight consecutive albums to have a chart-topping debut. The album featured appearances from artists such as Beyoncé, Ed Sheeran, Alicia Keys, Pink, Kehlani, and X Ambassadors.

Overall, reviews of the album were mixed. Some hard-core fans were disappointed by its heavy use of pop artists and reliance on rock music in production. In *Rolling Stone*, music critic Christopher Weingarten wrote, "The majority of *Revival* is, well, a revival: a collection of labyrinthine raps without much of a narrative arc. Lyrically, Eminem mainly falls back on old tricks. But what tricks they are: part Big Daddy Kane, part

> **"I'm critical of myself and I'm always trying to figure out how to do better."[6]**
>
> *–Eminem*

Eminem's tour for *Revival* took him to stops in Europe, including Hanover, Germany.

Eddie Van Halen, part Marquis de Sade. He can still be the same booger-flicking shock-rocker, just in a dirty old man's body."[7]

Other critics were harsher. "Production-wise, *Revival* is a trainwreck," wrote Dom Needham in the *Guardian*. "If Eminem thinks his verbal box of tricks can overcome the weakness of any backing track, his recent albums have demonstrated otherwise."[8] Some critics questioned whether Eminem's skills had begun to lessen.

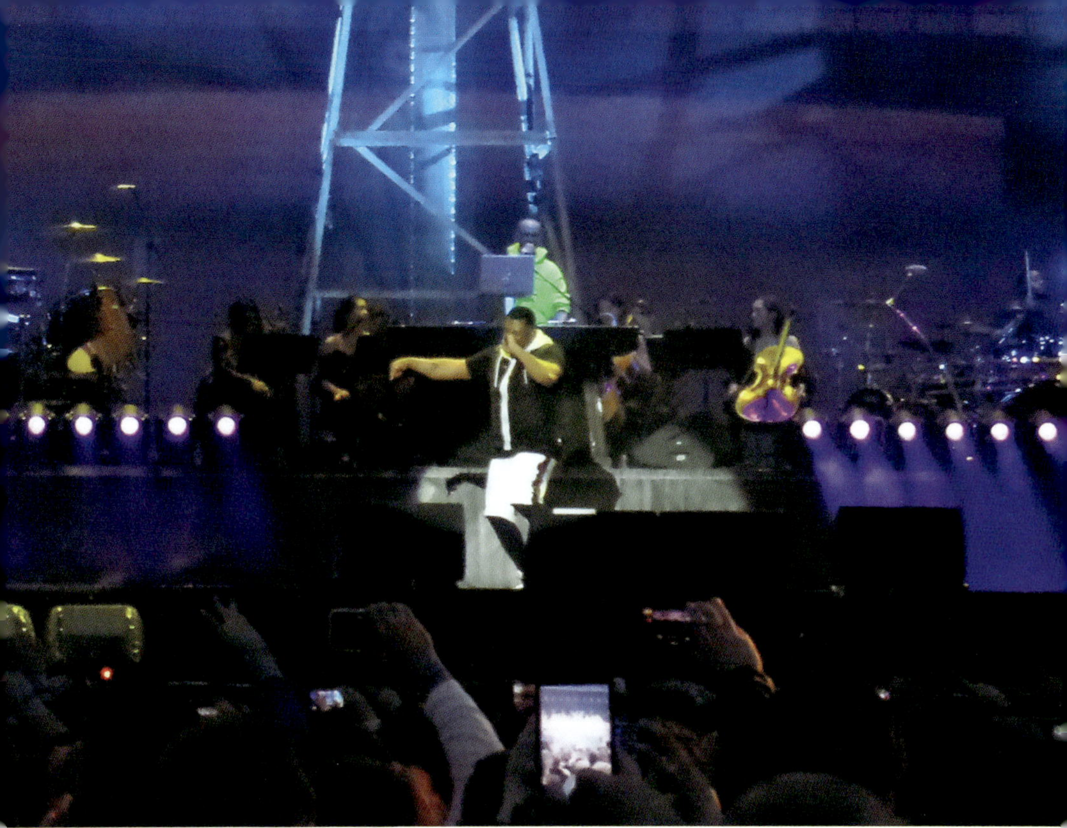

KAMIKAZE

Following the criticism of *Revival*, Eminem released a remix of the album's single "Chloraseptic," featuring 2 Chainz and Phresher. The remix mocked those who criticized the album. Eminem continued his response with the unannounced release of *Kamikaze* in 2018, which included more insults directed against his critics and other rappers.

The album performed well and opened at Number 1 in the United States and several other countries. The

> **"I started learning how to not be so angry about things, learning how to count my . . . blessings instead. By doing that, I've become a happier person, instead of all this self-loathing I was doing for a while."[10]**
>
> ***–Eminem on how his work had changed by 2018***

single "Venom," part of the soundtrack to the Marvel movie of the same name, was also popular. Eventually, the album sold more than one million copies.[9]

Critics gave *Kamikaze* mixed reviews. Some found it to be an improvement over Eminem's recent work and a return to earlier, more aggressive material. Others criticized it for not adapting to the modern sounds of hip-hop.

Like many of Eminem's albums, *Kamikaze* was not without controversy. The use of homophobic slurs offended some listeners. The release sparked feuds with several artists, including Lil Yachty, Machine Gun Kelly, and Ja Rule, all of whom Eminem insulted in the album's lyrics.

MUSIC TO BE MURDERED BY

Eminem surprised fans again with the release of his eleventh album, *Music to Be Murdered By*, in January 2020. It debuted at Number 1 on the *Billboard* 200 chart, his tenth consecutive album to do so. Like *Kamikaze*, *Music to Be Murdered By* included rants against the critics who bashed his previous work. Although it was a familiar formula, it seemed to be working for the rapper. "Lucky for Eminem (and much to the chagrin of his critics), he can rehash these tirades ad infinitum as long as he maintains a palpable level of vitriol, because his fans crave them, and they will ensure he remains a chart-topping phenomenon without ever having to release another good album," wrote music critic Brian Rolli for *Forbes* magazine.[11]

Eminem surprised his fans one more time with the release of 16 new songs on *Music to Be Murdered By—Side B* in December 2020. The album is a companion to his January release. The surprise release landed at Number 3 on the *Billboard* 200 chart, behind Taylor Swift's *Evermore* and Paul McCartney's *McCartney III*.

Chapter EIGHT

GETTING POLITICAL

Throughout his career, Eminem has been known as an artist who is not afraid to say just about anything and doesn't worry about who might be offended. In October 2017, he turned his sharp wit against President Donald Trump at the BET Hip-Hop Awards. The rapper filmed a more than four-minute video called "The Storm" that aired during the awards show. In the video, which was filmed in a Detroit parking lot, Eminem launched a pointed freestyle rap attack on President Trump. In his rhymes, he held little back. He accused Trump of being a racist, criticized him for taking extravagant golf trips, and slammed him for policies the rapper believed were harmful to the country. The rapper accused Trump of ignoring real tragedies in favor of tweeting.

In "The Storm," Eminem also called Trump out for being a hypocrite because Trump criticized the NFL's

During the presidency of Donald Trump, Eminem was outspoken about his opposition to Trump.

national anthem protests as disrespectful to the military while at the same time disparaging Senator John McCain for being captured during the Vietnam War (1954–1975). At the end of the video, Eminem issued an ultimatum to his fans. "Any fan of mine who's a supporter of his. I'm drawing in the sand a line. You're either for or against," he said.[1]

"CAMPAIGN SPEECH"

In October 2016, Eminem released the freestyle rap song "Campaign Speech." It was dropped on October 19, 2016, the same day as a presidential debate between Hillary Clinton and Donald Trump. In the nearly eight-minute song, Eminem uses puns and clever rhymes to share his opinion on several controversial hot topics, including Donald Trump, San Francisco 49ers quarterback Colin Kaepernick, mass murderer Dylann Roof, and Trayvon Martin's killer, George Zimmerman.

"THE STORM" GOES VIRAL

After the BET Hip-Hop Awards, "The Storm" went viral. Within hours, a YouTube clip of the video received 6.5 million views.[2] Reaction was swift. Several celebrities tweeted or posted their support of Eminem's video message on social media, including former San Francisco 49ers quarterback Colin Kaepernick, rap star Snoop Dogg, basketball star LeBron James, and more.

When asked about the reaction to "The Storm," Eminem said that he was not surprised. For him, most rap is meant to provoke a reaction from listeners. "But where I was coming from in that cypher was a genuine place in my heart. I [hesitate] to say [I have] hatred in my heart for him, but it's serious contempt. I do not like the guy," he says.[3]

Eminem's comments about Trump resulted in both support and criticism from the rapper's fans.

In a December 2017 interview, Eminem explained why he felt the need to speak out against the president. "I remember when he was first sniffing around politics, I thought, 'We've tried everything else, why not him?' Then—and I was watching it live—he had that speech where he said Mexico is sending us rapists and criminals. I got this feeling of 'what the f—?' From that point on, I knew it was going to be bad with him. What he's doing putting people against each other is scary. . . . His election was such a disappointment to me about the state of the country," he says.[4]

> **"All jokes aside, all punchlines aside, I'm trying to get a message out there about him. I want our country to be great too, I want it to be the best it can be, but it's not going to be that with him in charge."[6]**
>
> ***–Eminem talking about President Donald Trump***

Not everyone approved of Eminem's anti-Trump message. Some fans who were Trump supporters tweeted their disapproval of the rapper's political attacks. One fan tweeted, "I was a fan for many years now. #eminem asking for a line in the sand? Your officially a joke."[5] Despite the controversy, Eminem refused to change his position and doubled down on his anti-Trump message, even if it cost him professionally. "At the end of the day, if I did lose half my fan base, then so be it, because I feel like I stood up for what was right and I'm on the right side of this. I don't see how somebody could be middle class, [working hard] every single day, paycheck to paycheck, who thinks that that . . . billionaire is gonna help you," he said.[7]

"DARKNESS" AGAINST GUN VIOLENCE

In 2020, Eminem released the music video for the single "Darkness" from *Music to Be Murdered By*. In the video, the rapper urges fans to vote to change gun laws. In the video, Eminem takes on the persona of the 2017 Las Vegas shooter, who killed 58 people and injured hundreds more.[8] He raps about the moments leading up to the shooting. The video then features a graphic re-creation of the shooter firing from his Las Vegas hotel. Eminem mentions other deadly mass shootings in a series of sound bites. He asks fans when it will end and urges them to register to vote.

TARGETING OTHER POLITICIANS

While "The Storm" may have caught the attention of many people, it was not the first time Eminem had gotten political in his music and lyrics. He created lyrics at the expense of former president Bill Clinton and his wife, former secretary of state Hillary Clinton, on several songs, including "Role Model" on *The Slim Shady LP* and "Who Knew" on *The Marshall Mathers LP*. In a later

Eminem has used his platform to speak out about the Black Lives Matter movement and other issues and causes.

single, "Rap God" on *The Marshall Mathers LP 2*, Eminem targeted Bill Clinton's affair with White House intern Monica Lewinsky.

When President George W. Bush was in office, Eminem took aim once again through his music. He experimented with adding more political content to his raps. Punch lines became verses and evolved into entire songs. Songs like "Square Dance," "We as Americans," and "Public Enemy #1" took direct aim at President Bush and his Republican colleagues.

SECRET SERVICE INVESTIGATION

Eminem's anti-Bush messages drew the attention of the Secret Service. In the song "We as Americans," Eminem rapped about a dead president. The lyric drew the attention of the Secret Service as a possible threat to President Bush. In the song, Eminem sings, "F— money, I don't rap for dead presidents. I'd rather see the president dead."[9] Eminem's representatives explained the lyric used the word "president" as slang for money because former presidents are pictured on dollar bills.

REVIVAL CALLS OUT RACISM

Several tracks on 2017's *Revival* featured more political content. In "Untouchable," he raps about the Black Lives Matter movement, police

BLACK
LIVES
MATTER

WHAT HAPPENED IN CHARLOTTESVILLE?

In Charlottesville, Virginia, a months-long struggle had taken place over what to do with a statue of Confederate leader General Robert E. Lee. Many people believed that Confederate statues inappropriately celebrate the legacy of slavery and should be taken down. In 2017, the Charlottesville City Council voted to remove the statue and rename the park where it stood. On August 12, 2017, a "Unite the Right" rally was held in Charlottesville to protest the statue's removal. The rally turned deadly when a 20-year-old man drove his car into a crowd of counterprotesters, killing one woman and injuring 19 others. In a statement, President Trump stirred controversy by condemning the violence but not calling out the white nationalist and neo-Nazi hate groups who had been present.

brutality, and racism in the United States. He criticizes the country's racist history, rapping, "Throughout history, African-Americans have been treated like s—. And I admit that there have been times where it's been embarrassing to be a white boy."[10]

Throughout the album, Eminem rails against politicians, systemic racism, and more, with particular fury reserved for President Trump. In "Like Home," Eminem calls on his fans to come together against racism after protests over Confederate statues in Charlottesville, Virginia, turned deadly in 2017. He questions the president's decision to ban transgender people from the military and accuses him of watching and repeating Fox News like a parrot. Through his rap lyrics, Eminem urges Americans to stand up and fight for a more unified country.

Eminem has spoken out about the racist protesters who marched in Charlottesville, Virginia, in 2017.

UNLIKE ANY OTHER

Chapter NINE

For more than two decades, Eminem has thrilled fans and dismayed critics with his tongue-twisting, often vulgar, sharp-as-a-knife rap verses. After all of the albums, accolades, and controversy, Eminem has become a verified legend in the music industry and has left a lasting impact on both rap and the music industry as a whole.

BRINGING RAP MAINSTREAM

Since his widespread introduction to the music world with *The Slim Shady LP*, Eminem has helped bring rap and hip-hop music into the mainstream. He has been more commercially successful than any other hip-hop artist before him. In fact, Eminem is more than just a commercially successful rapper. He is one of the best-selling artists in the world, selling more than 100 million albums worldwide.[1]

Throughout his career, Eminem has challenged perceptions of what it means to be a rapper and has changed the world of hip-hop.

In the 2000s, Eminem was the best-selling artist from any genre. In addition, he landed two albums in that decade's top ten best sellers. *The Marshall Mathers LP* ranked fourth with 10,195,000 copies sold, while *The Eminem Show* ranked fifth with 9,789,000 albums sold.[2]

MARSHALL MATHERS FOUNDATION

In 2002, Eminem founded the Marshall Mathers Foundation. The foundation's goal is to help disadvantaged and at-risk youth in the Detroit area. The foundation is known for helping several boys' and girls' clubs and food banks in the region with fundraisers and donations. Because the rapper prefers to keep his charitable works private, the foundation serves as a channel for his personal charitable donations.

For his success over two decades, *Rolling Stone* magazine ranked Eminem Number 82 in its list of the 100 greatest artists of all time. Eminem's success proved that rap and hip-hop music could have mainstream appeal and be commercially successful. His success inspired other rappers and hip-hop artists to follow in his footsteps and pursue their own music-industry dreams.

UNIQUE FLOW AND DELIVERY

Over his two-decade career, Eminem has become known for his unique flow and delivery. He delivers his songs with almost manic speed and unique rhythms. Across songs and albums, he has used his different personas—Marshall Mathers, Eminem, and Slim Shady—to experiment with the pitch and speed of his lyrics and create a delivery style that is all his own.

Eminem's play with his flow and delivery influenced other rappers to also experiment with their flow and how they delivered their rhymes. Rapper Kendrick Lamar, who also changes personas and voices in his music, credits Eminem as having a significant influence on his career. In a 2016 interview he said, "I got my clarity just

EMINEM AND HAILIE

Throughout his career, Eminem has mentioned his daughter Hailie in more than 20 songs, including "Mockingbird," "Cleanin' Out My Closet," "When I'm Gone," and "Hailie's Song." In 2002, a young Hailie even provided vocals on two of her father's songs. Eminem credits his daughter with being his main source of drive and motivation. His fierce desire to protect and provide for her drove him to stay focused and keep working to push his career higher and higher. As an adult, Hailie graduated from college and became an up-and-coming social media influencer. She and Eminem have maintained a close relationship over the years.

Eminem's rapid-fire delivery and lyrical skills have won him millions of fans, including other top rappers.

studying Eminem when I was a kid. . . . The day I heard *The Marshall Mathers LP*, I was just like, How does that work? What is he doing? How is he putting his words together like that?"[3] Chance the Rapper is another artist who credits Eminem as an influence. "Eminem is one of my biggest influences in music. MMLP is where I got my flow from," he says.[4]

EARNING A PLACE IN HIP-HOP HISTORY

Before Eminem, white rappers had little credibility in the industry. While the Beastie Boys had enjoyed success in the 1980s, rappers like Vanilla Ice had become novelty acts. Then Eminem entered the rap and hip-hop scene. He earned respect by rising through Detroit's rap-battle circuit. He gained a following through his performance in the Rap Olympics. And he did it by telling his own story. "He took a chance at opening a door that was normally closed and he told a story that nobody had ever heard," says Denaun Porter of D12. "Em took the art of what hip hop

> **"Hip-hop's went through too many different transitions for anyone really to be the best rapper of all time."[5]**
>
> *–Eminem*

Eminem performed before a huge crowd of fans at the Bonnaroo music festival in 2018.

was and turned it into his thing, right? So it wasn't as if he took it and abused it, what he did was he took it and made it his own. He became a storyteller for white people and changed the way everybody looked at their own lives."[6]

Today there are many white rappers enjoying success, including G-Eazy and Machine Gun Kelly. According to Porter, Eminem was a trailblazer who earned the respect of the industry and made it easier for these artists and future white rappers to follow in the industry. "He changed the way people looked at a white person in the genre. He opened the door for every white rapper period. It was bigger than 3rd Bass and Vanilla Ice and Everlast, and all the others that came before him. He opened the door that much wider," says Porter.[7]

From Marshall Mathers III to Eminem to Slim Shady, there are many sides to the man known as Eminem. He's a comedic

ADE ME DO IT

Through accolades, controversies, and personal challenges, Eminem has developed a rap career that will stand the test of time.

rapper who can also write introspective rhymes. He's a celebrity who has won 15 Grammys, an Oscar, and numerous other awards, as well as a father who values his privacy. He may be rich and famous, but he's also struggled to overcome addiction and adversity to earn his place in rap history. Through it all, Eminem has cemented his status as one of rap's most legendary stars.

COVID RELIEF

During the COVID-19 pandemic in 2020, Eminem donated 400 meals to health-care workers and delivered the meals to two Detroit hospitals. He also donated a rare pair of Jordan 4 Retro Eminem Carhartt shoes for a raffle benefiting COVID-19 relief efforts. Additionally, Eminem announced with Twitter CEO Jack Dorsey that they had committed $1 million to help Detroit residents during the pandemic.[8]

TIMELINE

1972
Marshall Mathers III is born on October 17 to parents Debbie Mathers-Briggs and Marshall Mathers Jr.

1989
Eminem drops out of high school after failing ninth grade three times.

1995
Eminem's daughter, Hailie Jade Mathers, is born on December 25.

1996
Eminem releases his debut album, *Infinite*, under the independent Web Entertainment label.

1997
Eminem performs at the Los Angeles Rap Olympics, which leads to his meeting rap legend Dr. Dre.

1999
In February, Eminem releases *The Slim Shady LP*.

Eminem and longtime girlfriend Kimberly Scott marry in June.

2000
In May, Eminem releases *The Marshall Mathers LP*.

2001
Eminem and Kim divorce.

2002
Eminem releases *The Eminem Show*.

The movie *8 Mile* starring Eminem is released in theaters.

2003
The single "Lose Yourself" from *8 Mile* wins an Oscar for Best Original Song.

2004

Eminem releases *Encore*.

2006

Eminem and Kim remarry and divorce a few months later.

2009

Eminem releases *Relapse*, which follows his struggles with drug addiction.

2010

Eminem releases *Recovery*, which centers on his recovery from addiction.

2013

Eminem releases *The Marshall Mathers LP 2*, which critics praise as his best work in years.

2017

In October, Eminem's freestyle video "The Storm" airs on the BET Awards.

Eminem releases *Revival*.

2018

Eminem releases *Kamikaze*.

2020

Eminem releases *Music to Be Murdered By*, his tenth consecutive album to debut at Number 1 on the charts.

ESSENTIAL FACTS

FULL NAME

Marshall Mathers III

DATE OF BIRTH

October 17, 1972

PLACE OF BIRTH

Saint Joseph, Missouri

PARENTS

Debbie Mathers-Briggs and Marshall Mathers Jr.

EDUCATION

Eminem failed ninth grade three times and dropped out of high school.

CAREER HIGHLIGHTS

In a career that has spanned more than two decades, Eminem has enjoyed commercial and critical success. He has sold more than 100 million albums worldwide, with ten of his albums reaching Number 1 on the charts. In addition, Eminem has won 15 Grammy Awards, as well as an Academy Award for Best Original Song for "Lose Yourself." Eminem has become the best-selling hip-hop artist of all time and a legend in the world of rap.

ALBUMS

Infinite (1996), *The Slim Shady LP* (1999), *The Marshall Mathers LP* (2000), *The Eminem Show* (2002), *Encore* (2004), *Curtain Call: The Hits* (2005), *Relapse* (2009), *Recovery* (2010), *The Marshall Mathers LP 2* (2013), *Revival* (2017), *Kamikaze* (2018), *Music to Be Murdered By* (2020)

CONTRIBUTION TO HIP-HOP

Since his widespread introduction to the music world with *The Slim Shady LP*, Eminem has made rap and hip-hop more mainstream than ever before. His music has been more commercially successful than any other hip-hop artist before him. Eminem has become one of the best-selling artists in the world, selling more than 100 million albums worldwide. His songs have been praised as funny and clever, and the rhymes seem to flow effortlessly from his mouth. Eminem has become known as a lyrical master with the ability to put together words into bars with double and even triple meanings.

CONFLICTS

Throughout his career, Eminem's music has generated controversy. Family groups, gay rights activists, and women's groups have criticized Eminem's music for its profanity, glorification of drugs, violent imagery, homophobia, and misogyny. Eminem has never been afraid to comment on politics and current events through his music. He used several songs to criticize politicians, particularly President Donald Trump, and their policies. Eminem has gotten into feuds with a variety of other artists, including Machine Gun Kelly and Hotstylz.

QUOTE

"Slim Shady is a name for my temper or anger. Eminem is just the rapper, Slim Shady is the attitude behind him, and Marshall Mathers is who I am at the end of the day."

—*Eminem*

GLOSSARY

ADVERSITY

Difficult circumstances.

ALTER EGO

A persona that an artist might use for different projects.

BLACK LIVES MATTER

A political and social activist group that was developed by Black people in the United States in 2013; the group campaigns to reduce violence and racism against Black people.

DEMO

A sound recording that is used to show off an artist to record producers.

EXTENDED PLAY (EP)

A musical recording of several songs, longer than a single but shorter than an album.

FLOW

The rhymes and rhythms of a song's lyrics and how they interact with each other.

FREESTYLING

Rapping lyrics that are made up by the performer on the spot.

HOMOPHOBIA

Fear of and hostility toward gay people.

LONG PLAY (LP)

A full-length album of music.

MC

A person who speaks over a beat; interchangeable with "rapper."

MISOGYNY

Hatred of or contempt for women.

PLATINUM

An award, given by the Recording Industry Association of America (RIAA), that represents huge sales—500,000 albums for gold, one million for platinum, and two million or more for multiplatinum.

PROCLIVITY

A tendency.

PRODUCER

The person who supervises the sampling, mixing, and recording of music and also guides the performer.

RECORD LABEL

A company that promotes and publishes an artist's music.

REMIX

A new and different version of a previous recording.

SOUNDTRACK

A collection of music that accompanies a film.

WRITER'S BLOCK

A condition in which an artist feels unable to develop new work.

ADDITIONAL RESOURCES

SELECTED BIBLIOGRAPHY

Bozza, Anthony. *Not Afraid: The Evolution of Eminem*. Hachette, 2019.

Marchese, David. "In Conversation: Eminem," *Vulture*, Dec. 2017, vulture.com. Accessed 26 May 2021.

Touré. "Eminem: The Rolling Stone Interview," *Rolling Stone*, 25 Nov. 2004, rollingstone.com. Accessed 26 May 2021.

FURTHER READINGS

Cummings, Judy Dodge. *Hip-Hop Culture*. Abdo, 2018.

Kallen, Stuart A. *Rap and Hip-Hop*. ReferencePoint, 2020.

Lusted, Marcia Amidon. *Hip-Hop Music*. Abdo, 2018.

ONLINE RESOURCES

Booklinks
NONFICTION NETWORK
FREE! ONLINE NONFICTION RESOURCES

To learn more about Eminem, please visit **abdobooklinks.com** or scan this QR code. These links are routinely monitored and updated to provide the most current information available.

MORE INFORMATION

For more information on this subject, contact or visit the following organizations:

THE GRAMMY MUSEUM
800 W. Olympic Blvd.
Los Angeles, CA 90015
213-725-5700
grammymuseum.org

The Grammy Museum is an interactive, educational museum focused on the history and winners of the Grammy Awards.

RECORDING INDUSTRY ASSOCIATION OF AMERICA (RIAA)
1025 F St. NW, Tenth Floor
Washington, DC 20004
202-775-0101
riaa.com

The Recording Industry Association of America (RIAA) is the trade organization that supports and promotes the major music companies.

UNIVERSAL HIP HOP MUSEUM
610 Exterior St.
Bronx, NY 10451
347-454-2793
uhhm.org

The Universal Hip Hop Museum in the Bronx celebrates and preserves the history of local and global hip-hop music and culture to inspire, empower, and promote understanding.

SOURCE NOTES

CHAPTER 1. DISCOVERY AT THE RAP OLYMPICS

1. Anthony Bozza. *Whatever You Say I Am: The Life and Times of Eminem*. Transworld Digital, 2010. 22.

2. Bozza, *Whatever You Say I Am*, 22.

3. Bozza, *Whatever You Say I Am*, 22.

4. Bozza, *Whatever You Say I Am*, 23–24.

5. Bozza, *Whatever You Say I Am*, 24.

6. Joe Tayson. "The Moment Dr. Dre Discovered Eminem." *Far Out*, Apr. 2021, faroutmagazine.co.uk. Accessed 29 July 2021.

7. Sam Moore. "Watch Eminem and Dr. Dre Recall the First Time They Met and Explain How They Wrote 'My Name Is.'" *NME*, 12 July 2017, nme.com. Accessed 29 July 2021.

8. Nick Hasted. *The Dark Story of Eminem*. Omnibus Press, 2003. 74.

CHAPTER 2. THE EARLY YEARS

1. "Eminem's Incredible Rise to Stardom." *CBS News*, 7 Oct. 2010, cbsnews.com. Accessed 29 July 2021.

2. "Eminem's Incredible Rise to Stardom."

3. Charles Aaron. "The Slim Shady LP at 20: Read Our 1999 Interview with Eminem." *Spin*, 22 Feb. 2019, spin.com. Accessed 29 July 2021.

4. Kyle Eustice. "Eminem Talks 1st Dr. Dre Impression." *HipHopDX*, 22 Aug. 2018, hiphopdx.com. Accessed 29 July 2021.

5. "One Horrific Moment in Eminem's Life Made Him the Rapper That He Is Today." *Joe*, n.d., joe.ie. Accessed 29 July 2021.

CHAPTER 3. RAP BATTLES AND PERSONAL TROUBLES

1. Robert Hilburn. "Has He No Shame?" *Los Angeles Times*, 14 May 2000, latimes.com. Accessed 29 July 2021.

2. "Eminem." *Biography*, 27 Apr. 2017, biography.com. Accessed 29 July 2021.

3. Nick Hasted. *The Dark Story of Eminem*. Omnibus Press, 2003. 44.

4. Hasted, *The Dark Story of Eminem*, 30.

5. Charles Aaron. "The Slim Shady LP at 20: Read Our 1999 Interview with Eminem." *Spin*, 22 Feb. 2019, spin.com. Accessed 29 July 2021.

6. "Eminem's Incredible Rise to Stardom." *CBS News*, 7 Oct. 2010, cbsnews.com. Accessed 29 July 2021.

7. M. L. Elrick. "Eminem's Dirty Secrets." *Salon*, 26 July 2000, salon.com. Accessed 29 July 2021.

8. Anthony Bozza. "Eminem Blows Up." *Rolling Stone*, 29 Apr. 1999, rollingstone.com. Accessed 29 July 2021.

9. Hasted, *The Dark Story of Eminem*, 53.

10. Hilburn, "Has He No Shame?"

CHAPTER 4. "I'M SLIM SHADY"

1. Nick Hasted. *The Dark Story of Eminem*. E-book, Omnibus Press, 2011.
2. Max Bell. "American Psycho: Eminem's *Marshall Mathers LP* at 20." *Spin*, 22 May 2020, spin.com. Accessed 29 July 2021.
3. Robert Hilburn. "Has He No Shame?" *Los Angeles Times*, 14 May 2000, latimes.com. Accessed 29 July 2021.
4. Anthony Bozza. "Eminem Blows Up." *Rolling Stone*, 29 Apr. 1999, rollingstone.com. Accessed 29 July 2021.
5. Stephen Thomas Erlewine. "The Slim Shady LP—Eminem." *AllMusic*, n.d., allmusic.com. Accessed 29 July 2021.
6. Mark Beaumont. "The Story of Eminem's Marshall Mathers LP." *Independent*, 23 May 2020, independent.co.uk. Accessed 29 July 2021.
7. Will Lavin. "20 Years of Eminem's 'The Slim Shady LP.'" *NME*, 25 Feb. 2019, nme.com. Accessed 29 July 2021.
8. Hilburn, "Has He No Shame?"
9. "The Slim Shady LP." *Billboard*, n.d., billboard.com. Accessed 29 July 2021.
10. Erika Ramirez and Brad Wete. "Eminem's 30 Biggest Billboard Hot 100 Hits." *Billboard*, 17 Oct. 2017, billboard.com. Accessed 29 July 2021.

CHAPTER 5. WORLDWIDE SUCCESS AND BACKLASH

1. "Oh Yes, It's Shady's Night." *Eminem World*, 28 Apr. 2000, eminemworld.com. Accessed 29 July 2021.
2. Greg Kot. "The Rap That Dre Built." *Chicago Tribune*, 2 July 2000, chicagotribune.com. Accessed 29 July 2021.
3. "Billboard 200, Week of May 27, 2000." *Billboard*, May 2000, billboard.com. Accessed 29 July 2021.
4. "On with the 'Show': Eminem Album an Instant No. 1." *Billboard*, 30 May 2002, billboard.com. Accessed 29 July 2021.
5. Gary Trust. "Eminem's 20 Billboard Hot 100 Top 10s, From 'The Real Slim Shady' to 'Killshot.'" *Billboard*, 25 Sept. 2018, billboard.com. Accessed 29 July 2021.
6. Max Bell. "American Psycho: Eminem's 'Marshall Mathers' LP at 20." *Yahoo*, 22 May 2020, money.yahoo.com. Accessed 29 July 2021.
7. Touré. "Eminem's 'The Marshall Mathers LP' Album Review." *Rolling Stone*, 6 July 2000, rollingstone.com. Accessed 29 July 2021.
8. Rob Mancini. "Eminem Targeted at Senate Hearing." *MTV News*, 13 Sept. 2000, mtv.com. Accessed 29 July 2021.
9. Brian Hiatt. "Eminem's Grammy Nods Draw Protests from Women's Gay Groups." *MTV*, 4 Jan. 2001, mtv.com. Accessed 29 July 2021.
10. Elton John. "Eminem." *Interview*, 7 Dec. 2017, interviewmagazine.com. Accessed 29 July 2021.
11. Matthew Neale. "Eminem Celebrates 'Without Me' Video Reaching a Billion Views with HD Version." *NME*, 11 Nov. 2020, nme.com. Accessed 29 July 2021.
12. Alan Light. "Behind Blue Eyes: Spin's 2002 Eminem Cover Story." *Spin*, 31 May 2017, spin.com. Accessed 29 July 2021.
13. Christina Fuoco. "'8 Mile' Director Lauds Eminem." *Rolling Stone*, 24 Oct. 2002, rollingstone.com. Accessed 29 July 2021.
14. Jeff Dickerson. "Eminem's Feature Film Debut, '8 Mile,' Breaks Box Office Records." *Michigan Daily*, 12 Nov. 2002, michigandaily.com. Accessed 29 July 2021.
15. "8 Mile." *IMDB*, n.d., imdb.com. Accessed 29 July 2021.

SOURCE NOTES CONTINUED

CHAPTER 6. *RELAPSE* AND *RECOVERY*

1. Anthony Bozza. *Not Afraid: The Evolution of Eminem*. Hachette, 2019. 13.
2. Bozza, *Not Afraid*, 21.
3. Bozza, *Not Afraid*, 36.
4. Bozza, *Not Afraid*, 42.
5. Bozza, *Not Afraid*, 41.
6. Bozza, *Not Afraid*, 31.
7. Bozza, *Not Afraid*, 51.

CHAPTER 7. NEW MUSIC

1. Nadeska Alexis. "Eminem Drops VMA Surprise: New Album Release Date Is Set!" *MTV*, 25 Aug. 2013, mtv.com. Accessed 29 July 2021.
2. Edna Gunderson. "Review: Eminem's 'MMLP2' Returns to Original's Wild Wit." *USA Today*, 1 Nov. 2013, usatoday.com. Accessed 29 July 2021.
3. Anthony Bozza. *Not Afraid: The Evolution of Eminem*. Hachette, 2019. 171.
4. Keith Caulfield. "Eminem's 'Marshall Mathers LP 2' Scores Second-Biggest Debut of Year." *Billboard*, 12 Nov. 2013, billboard.com. Accessed 29 July 2021.
5. Emma Nolan. "Machine Gun Kelly and Eminem's Feud Explained." *Newsweek*, 22 Dec. 2020, newsweek.com. Accessed 29 July 2021.
6. David Marchese. "In Conversation: Eminem." *Vulture*, Dec. 2017, vulture.com. Accessed 29 July 2021.
7. Christopher Weingarten. "Review: Eminem Is Raw, Honest and Compelling as Ever on 'Revival.'" *Rolling Stone*, 15 Dec. 2017, rollingstone.com. Accessed 29 July 2021.
8. Dom Needham. "Eminem: Revival Review—Puns and Witless Beats in a Total Rejection of Hip-Hop." *Guardian*, 16 Dec. 2017, theguardian.com. Accessed 29 July 2021.
9. Samantha Maine. "Eminem's 'Kamikaze' Has Now Gone Platinum." *NME*, 23 Oct. 2018, nme.com. Accessed 29 July 2021.
10. Brian Mockenhaupt. "Eminem: What I've Learned." *Esquire*, 18 Dec. 2008, esquire.com. Accessed 29 July 2021.
11. Brian Rolli. "'Music to Be Murdered By' Is Proof Eminem Never Needs to Release Another Great Album." *Forbes*, 22 Jan. 2020, forbes.com. Accessed 29 July 2021.

CHAPTER 8. GETTING POLITICAL

1. Eugene Scott. "It's Not Surprising That Eminem Doesn't Like Trump, but Here's Why His Rap about Him Is Resonating." *Washington Post*, 11 Oct. 2017, washingtonpost.com. Accessed 29 July 2021.
2. Adam Graham. "Kaepernick, Others React to Eminem's Trump Freestyle." *Detroit News*, 11 Oct. 2017, detroitnews.com. Accessed 29 July 2021.
3. Dan Rys. "Eminem and New Def Jam CEO Paul Rosenberg on Early 'Broke Days,' Courting Controversy and Hip-Hop's Future." *Billboard*, 25 Jan. 2018, billboard.com. Accessed 29 July 2021.
4. David Marchese. "In Conversation: Eminem." *Vulture*, Dec. 2017, vulture.com. Accessed 29 July 2021.
5. Caitlin Kelley. "Trump-Supporting Eminem Fans Express Outrage on Twitter over Rapper's Anti-Trump Freestyle." *Billboard*, 11 Oct. 2017, billboard.com. Accessed 29 July 2021.

6. Marchese, "In Conversation: Eminem."

7. Rys, "Eminem and New Def Jam CEO Paul Rosenberg."

8. Kieran Corcoran, Sinéad Baker, and David Choi. "The FBI Has Closed Its Investigation of the Las Vegas Mass Shooting." *Business Insider*, 29 Jan. 2019, businessinsider.com. Accessed 29 July 2021.

9. "Secret Service Checks Eminem's 'Dead President' Lyric." *CNN*, 6 Dec. 2003, edition.cnn.com. Accessed 29 July 2021.

10. Paul Bowler. "Power and Politics: Eminem on the Road to 'Revival.'" *UDiscoverMusic*, 15 Dec. 2020, udiscovermusic.com. Accessed 29 July 2021.

CHAPTER 9. UNLIKE ANY OTHER

1. "Eminem." *Shady Records*, n.d., shadyrecords.com. Accessed 29 July 2021.

2. Daniel Kreps. "Eminem and the Beatles: The Top-Selling Artists of the 2000s." *Rolling Stone*, 9 Dec. 2009, rollingstone.com. Accessed 29 July 2021.

3. "Kendrick Lamar Meets Rick Rubin and They Have an Epic Conversation." *YouTube*, uploaded by GQ, 20 Oct. 2016, youtube.com.

4. Remy Gelenidze. "Young Rappers Influenced & Inspired by Eminem, from Kendrick to Chance The Rapper." *Southpawer*, 13 May 2015, southpawer.com. Accessed 29 July 2021.

5. Joe Price. "Eminem on Why It's Hard to Choose 'Anyone Really to Be the Best Rapper of All Time' Anymore." *Complex*, 30 Dec. 2020, complex.com. Accessed 29 July 2021.

6. Will Lavin. "20 Years of Eminem's 'The Slim Shady LP.'" *NME*, 25 Feb. 2019, nme.com. Accessed 29 July 2021.

7. Lavin, "20 Years of Eminem's 'The Slim Shady LP.'"

8. Adam Graham. "Eminem, Big Sean, Rihanna Help Raise Millions in COVID-19 Relief Funds." *Detroit News*, 10 May 2020, detroitnews.com. Accessed 29 July 2021.

INDEX

ABOUT THE AUTHOR

CARLA MOONEY

Carla Mooney is the author of many books for young adults and children. She lives in Pittsburgh, Pennsylvania, with her husband and three children.